Better Dancing

Better Dancing

Lyndon B. Wainwright

Photographs by Jack Blake

Kaye & Ward, Kingswood

First published by
Kaye & Ward Ltd
The Windmill Press
Kingswood, Tadworth, Surrey
1983

ISBN 0 7182 1476 5

All enquiries and requests relevant
to this title should be sent
to the publishers at the above
address and not to the printer

Printed in England by
Whitstable Litho Ltd.,
Whitstable, Kent

CONTENTS

The hold taken by better dancers.
Note the more erect carriage and the slight backward
lean of the lady.

INTRODUCTION

Sooner or later nearly everyone has to make some attempt at ballroom dancing. Ballroom dancing? Well, I mean any sort of social dancing done to popular music. So this includes disco dances, Latin dances such as cha cha cha and samba and traditional ballroom dances like waltz and quickstep. In this book I will include those dances which you would find useful if you went to a dinner and dance or attended a social at which dancing took place.

Millions, and I do mean millions, have enjoyed the dances which will be explained in these pages. It is a marvellous pastime. The beginner can get great enjoyment from quite simple dancing, while there is enough depth and scope to please those who want to develop their dancing to the highest possible levels, no matter how demanding they are.

Dancing is a wonderful way to keep fit and those who dance also learn to stand and breathe well.

What is dancing? It is no more than some fairly simple physical movements made in time to music. Many of the dances described are based upon walking to music. Whenever you hear a military band and see soldiers marching to music, they are responding to the music in a manner which could well be regarded as dancing. Most of us are able to march in time to music and for those who can the musical aspects should present no difficulties and if you cannot, do not despair, it is possible to be trained to hear the beat in the music.

Most of the dances are dances for two people, a boy and a girl, and dancing is one of the nicest ways to get to know the opposite sex.

Once you have learnt to move in time to music and to perform a few simple steps, you will find that you get great enjoyment and satisfaction from dancing. This is why so many people who start to dance in order to be socially acceptable find that they really like the feeling of dancing and responding to music. After all it is one of the most natural of instincts, and we can continue to dance and enjoy dancing for its own sake for the rest of our lives.

It is a pastime you will never regret starting which will give you enjoyment and help keep you fit for a very considerable time.

When learning to dance, firstly you should cast out from your mind any ideas about dancing you may have gathered beforehand. Secondly you must remember, at all times, that you are learning to dance for fun and you must try not to be too serious about it. It is inevitable that you will make some mistakes to start with and you must not allow these to upset you. If you can laugh when you have made a mistake, half the difficulties of learning will evaporate.

In most dances there are a number of different things which have to be learnt. There is the pattern of the steps and there is the rhythm or the 'timing' for each step. Where appropriate you also have to learn hand and arm movements and how to guide your partner into her steps should you be a man, or to follow your partner's lead should you be a lady.

How does one learn from a book? It would be foolish to pretend that it is as easy to learn from a book as it would be if you had your own instructor. However, it is certainly possible to learn sufficient to enable you to venture on the floor in a number of dances and to get much enjoyment. I feel sure once you have started you will want to pursue this further and I can do no more than suggest that once the ice is broken you should consider approaching a local dance school to join one of its classes.

HOW TO LEARN

KEEPING IT SIMPLE

I have tried to keep my approach simple and for that reason have avoided intricate details which could confuse beginners. All good teachers vary technique to enable the learning process to be efficient and I have done the same. If you decide to pursue dancing further, competent teachers can soon introduce more advanced step movements.

Fashions in clothes change but it is worth saying that both lady and gentlemen should wear light shoes and that for most dances the girls will find it easier if they have a heel to their shoe rather than a flat shoe.

Finally, you will all have seen expert dancers performing on the television and it may be that in years to come you might aspire to those giddy heights. However we are mainly concerned with learning the basics of social dancing; and fortunately, there is just as much enjoyment in dancing for the beginner as there is for the more advanced and experienced dancer.

ABOUT LEARNING

There are three sorts of dance which we will include in this book. Some are called contact dances in which the man takes hold of the lady and holds her close to him throughout. This is the hold which will be used for the waltz and we will describe it later. Another sort of dance is that in which the man holds the lady, but at some little distance away from him. In this category is the cha cha cha and jive. While the third form is that of solo dancing like disco where there is often no hold between man and partner.

The "closed" hold for waltz, social foxtrot, quickstep, etc.

ABOUT THE MUSIC

Before you start any dance you will need to know what the appropriate dance is for the music being played. This is dictated by the rhythm of the music and the speed at which it is played (called the tempo). There are exceptions but most of the tunes to which you will dance are written with four beats to the bar or with three beats to the bar. Examples of music written in four beats to the bar (4/4 or common time) are 'Dancing in the rain', 'If you knew Susie', 'As time goes by' and 'The way we were'. Music in 3/4 time is invariably that of waltzes such as 'Beautiful dreamer', 'Scarborough fair' and so on.

The commonest of all music is that written in 4/4 time and here the beginner is lucky because to this music there is one dance which can be used in all circumstances. We call it social foxtrot and not only is it suitable for most music in 4/4 time, whether it be fairly quick or very slow, but it is also suitable for dancing in crowded conditions such as the traditional cafe or club dance floor.

10

THE 'CLOSED' HOLD (as for the waltz)

Before we start learning the dance itself, let us consider how the couple should stand. Both man and lady should stand up and avoid slouching. The lady stands close to the man and a tiny fraction to her left. The man places his right hand on the lady's back just below the shoulder blade and holds the lady's right hand comfortably in his left hand somewhere level with his chin and with the elbow held slightly away from the body at a comfortable angle. This hold is much more casual than that you will see better dancers use, but we suggest you do not try anything more elaborate at the start.

LEADING

It is quite natural for beginners to worry about whether they are going to tread on their partner's feet. The man's ability to 'lead' is important and provided you stand up well and keep contact between you and your partner's body, leading is more a question of confidence than any special ability. If you wish to step forward with your left foot it is necessary for you first to settle your weight firmly on your right foot.

Let us try a little exercise. Stand with your feet five to seven centimetres (two or three inches) apart with the weight felt equally between both feet. Sway the weight over to the right foot until you feel the left foot free of the floor. You are now ready to move the left foot forward, side or back. If you have hold of a partner and do exactly the same as we have just done, your partner should also feel your weight settle over to your right, that is her left, and she should allow her weight to move with yours. This will leave her right foot free to move when you use your left foot.

Now if you move off in the direction in which you wish to move making sure that the body moves with the foot and that you do not stick out the foot first and then follow with the body, your partner will be compelled to move in the corresponding direction. However, until you have a good deal of experience do not take steps which are too long. Restrict yourselves to steps which are shorter than those you would use when walking, although they have the same character as those you would use when walking.

This is the basis of leading and following in all contact dances. Once you are moving it is important to take the weight fully on each step in turn and not to try to rush matters. This is another reason for keeping the steps not too long. You need to be quite expert before you can stride out with the length of step used by experienced dancers.

WHAT IS A STEP?

Throughout this book we write about 'steps' and dancers use two meanings to the word step.

Correctly, a step is commonly the movement of one foot from one position to its next position. However, groups of such steps such as the six steps of the right turn (or natural turn) in the waltz, are often called 'steps' instead of the more correct term 'figure'.

We need to think a little about individual steps and, in particular, backward steps.

We are all used to walking forward and forward steps in dancing do not differ much from walking. However, moving backwards is something of which most of us have little, if any, practice.

In the dances where man and lady stand with body contact (such as waltz and quickstep) some attention needs to be given to how backward walks should be taken. The hips and body weight are held over the supporting foot as long as possible.

Thus, consider what happens when you step backwards with the right foot. Start with the full weight felt over the left foot. This should make it possible to swing the right foot forward or back. When stepping back with the right foot the weight is kept on the left foot while the right leg is swung backwards. It is important that as the right foot moves backward the right ankle is straightened so that the right toes are pushed backwards.

If someone stands behind you as you step back he should see the sole of the right shoe.

This action allows the hips to be kept forward over the supporting foot -in this case the left foot. It also gets the toes back out of harm's way and makes it much more certain that you will not get your toes trodden on.

When the back foot reaches the position it is to move to it acts as a spring to control the pace or rate at which the weight is moved from the front foot and on to it.

Back Walk
Note how the lady, who is moving back, reaches back with toes, of the rear foot.

It is very helpful if the foot is flexible, for this will assist in avoiding a sudden fall backwards of the weight on to the back foot. The back foot acts as a shock absorber and smooths out backward movement.

Both man and lady need to think about back steps but it is perhaps more important for the lady, for a good use of the back foot helps her to follow the lead of the man.

FOLLOWING DESCRIPTIONS

When steps are given in the various figures to be taught, I will be asking you to 'step forward' or 'step back' or to 'step to side'. There is nothing difficult about these instructions but one little point needs to be explained.

Stand facing the nearest wall with the weight felt on the right foot. Now step to side with the left foot. This will leave you with your feet apart and both feet the same distance from the wall. This is the position you will

reach at the end of all steps to the side, no matter what has gone before. In other words, the step taken to the side is moved to a position to the side of the supporting foot.

Try this same action now after you have taken a forward step. Again face towards the nearest wall and take a step forward with the right foot. At the end of this step the right foot is forward in front of the left foot just as at the end of one walking step. If from this position I ask you to step to side with left foot, the left foot is moved to a position level with the right foot (the same distance from the wall) and about half a metre (one and a half feet) to the side.

This position which you have reached is the same as if you had started with the feet together before the side step was taken. What you should not do at the end of a forward step if then stepping to the side is merely to move the left foot sideways without bringing it up level with the supporting foot. This latter movement is awkward but sometimes beginners get confused about the action of side steps.

The instruction given describes the position reached at the end of one step at all times

14

MORE ABOUT THE MUSIC

As we have mentioned the music dictates the dance you are going to perform. Each dance has its own characteristic music and we have to set down the amount of music taken up by each step of each figure.

Any way of counting this — which we call the rhythm — which conveys what is needed is acceptable. If it was the case 'yackity yak' would be quite adequate. However, so that you know how long each step should take we must give this in more detail.

Waltz music has three beats to the bar, and the first is emphasised by the band and if you listen to good waltz music you should not find it difficult to pick out this stronger beat. You can then count the music 'one, two, three' and so on. In the same way the simple waltz figures are counted exactly the same, that is 'one, two, three'.

Sometimes four steps are fitted into one bar of waltz music and this can be done in many ways though in the simpler figures it is done by taking two steps in the time normally occupied by the second beat of music. When this happens instead of counting 'one, two, three' we count 'one, two, and, three' in order to fit the four counts into three beats the count of 'two and' are hurried so that each only occupies half of one beat. The beat value for each step is then:- one, half, half, one.

In dances written in 4/4 time, that is four beats to the bar, the emphasized beats are in foxtrot and quickstep the first and third. They are not so strongly emphasized as the waltz first beat but nevertheless can be heard if you listen carefully. In such dances we have commonly two sorts of steps in the figures. One type is a slow step which takes up two beats and the other is a quick step which takes up one beat. It would be possible for you to have four quick steps in a bar and in more advanced dancing this is quite usual but, for a little while, you will always find that your quick steps are interspersed with slow ones. The bars of music in 4/4 time for beginners are usually either slow, slow or slow, quick, quick or quick, quick, slow.

Can you think of the tune of Jingle Bells? The words Jingle Bells near the start of the music occupy one bar of music. You will remember that the words are repeated twice 'Jingle Bells, Jingle Bells'. This is two bars of music and represents a rhythm of quick, quick, slow, quick, quick, slow.

In this case 'Jin' is equivalent to quick, 'gle' is equivalent to quick, 'bells' is equivalent to slow. For those of you who understand music we print these two bars below, together with their appropriate count if we were dancing to them.

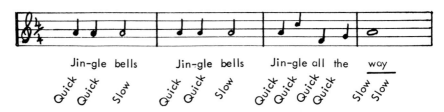

This use of Jingle Bells as an illustration is merely to help you understand how long quick and slow steps take. In practice slow and quick steps do not have to fit precisely to melodic lines, but have merely to fit to the bars of music.

Until you have a good deal of experience slow steps will always start on either the first or third beat of the bar and never on the second or fourth beat and you will always have quick steps coming in pairs and not singly.

JOINING FIGURES TOGETHER

In practice dances consist of individual figures, as described in this book, joined together one after another. In some dances this is simple for the figures are constructed so that any figure can follow any other figure. At the level covered by this book this applies to the cha cha cha.

However, in most dances the man has the responsibility of selecting one figure after another joining them together to form a continuous sequence.

This is largely a matter of experience, but I will be giving groupings of figures in each dance at appropriate points in the text.

FIRST STEPS

INTRODUCTION TO SOCIAL FOXTROT

The first dance to learn is the social foxtrot. There are many reasons for this but perhaps the most important is because this is a dance you will find throughout the world.

It can be done to a variety of types of music, it needs very little space, and it is probably the world's commonest dance. Wherever you may go either on holiday or travelling for any other reason, this is a dance you will be able to perform and which your partner will be able to follow.

It can be danced to any music written in 4/4 time, that is to say music with four beats or accents per bar. Musicians sometimes call this common time.

First we will learn the basic movement. I will explain this in two stages, first without any turn and then adding a little turn to it.

If you are fortunate enough to be learning with a partner, start facing your partner and with your hands resting lightly on your partner's shoulders. This will enable both of you to see how your steps fit with your partner's.

If you do not have a partner, it is not a bad idea to hold the book in both hands in front of you when, poor substitute that it is, you can regard the book as your partner.

The man starts facing the nearest wall but a metre or two away from it, while the lady stands in front of and facing the man so she has her back towards the nearest wall.

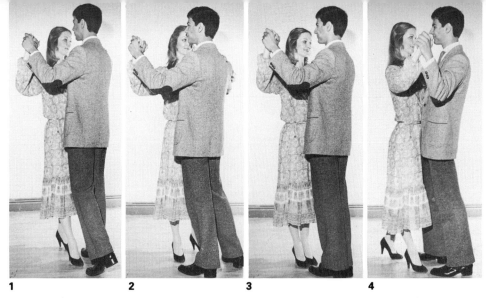

1 2 3 4

Quarter Turns, Social Foxtrot Steps 1-8

BASIC MOVEMENT

Man's Steps

1. Right foot forward.	Slow
2. Left foot to side.	Quick
3. Right foot closes to left foot.	Quick
4. Left foot back.	Slow
5. Right foot back.	Slow
6. Left foot to side.	Quick
7. Right foot closes to left foot.	Quick
8. Left foot forward.	Slow

Lady's Steps

1. Left foot back.	Slow
2. Right foot to side.	Quick
3. Left foot closes to right foot.	Quick
4. Right foot forward.	Slow
5. Left foot forward.	Slow
6. Right foot to side.	Quick
7. Left foot closes to right foot.	Quick
8. Right foot back.	Slow

5   6   7   8

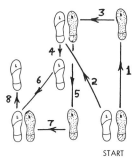

WALL

Social Foxtrot
MAN   basic movement

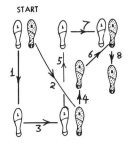

Social Foxtrot
LADY   basic movement

WALL

When you are sure you have mastered the steps of the basic movement take hold of your partner in the hold described in the section 'About Learning' and try what you have learnt so far.

BASIC MOVEMENT WITH TURN *(quarter turns)*

We are now going to use the same basic movement but add to it a little turn. On steps 1, 2 and 3 there is a little turn to the right — more about this in a moment — on step 4 there is no turn whilst on steps 5, 6 and 7 there is a little turn to the left. No turn on step 8.

Because we are turning we do not start facing straight towards the nearest wall. If the man will face the nearest wall and turn a little to his left so that he is now looking slanting at the wall (about 45 degrees for those mathematically inclined) this is the correct starting direction. The lady of course again faces the man and she will now have her back to the wall in a slanting direction.

Man's Steps with Turn

1.	Right foot forward starting to turn right.	Slow
2.	Left foot to side still turning right.	Quick
3.	Right foot closes to left foot still turning right so that the man is now facing straight towards the wall.	Quick
4.	Left foot back.	Slow
5.	Right foot back starting to turn to the left.	Slow
6.	Left foot to side still turning to left.	Quick
7.	Right foot closes to left foot still turning to left so that the man is now again facing slanting towards the wall.	Quick
8.	Left foot forward	Slow

The man has made just a little turn first to the right and then to the left. Sometimes pupils get confused about which is a right turn and which is a left turn. Shall we check?

If you face the wall and place some object on your right hand side and turn your body the shortest way so that you are able to look at the object, then you have turned to the right. This can happen while you are either stepping forward, backwards or sideways and is always a right hand turn irrespective of the direction of the step.

20

So, to repeat, if you turn to look towards objects on your right hand side you are turning right. It follows that if you turn to look towards objects on your left hand side you are turning left.

Now let us go through the lady's steps for this figure with turn.

Lady's Steps with Turn

1. Left foot back starting to turn to right.   Slow
2. Right foot to side still turning to right.   Quick
3. Left foot closes to right foot still turning to right, lady now has her back to the nearest wall.   Quick
4. Right foot forward.   Slow
5. Left foot forward starting to turn to left.   Slow
6. Right foot to side still turning to left.   Quick
7. Left foot closes to right foot still turning to left, lady is now backing in a slanting direction to the nearest wall.   Quick
8. Right foot back.   Slow

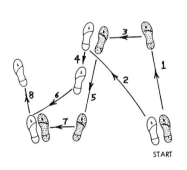

Social Foxtrot
MAN basic movement
with turn

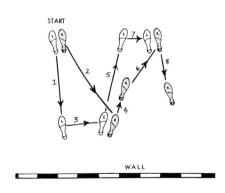

Social Foxtrot
LADY basic movement
with turn

In the descriptions we have given only a little turn for both lady and man. They both turn the same amount and remain facing each other throughout the figure. It is possible to turn more than we have given. Indeed twice as much on each half will be much more rewarding for you if you can manage it.

When you have completed the whole basic movement then it can be repeated so that when the man finishes the movement by stepping forward on his left foot, it leaves him ready to step forward again with the right foot for step 1 of the same figure. The figure when repeated will take you along the room, the general direction of the figure remaining parallel to the wall.

What on earth to do when you come to a corner?

Corners are not so much of a problem as you might imagine. When you are getting near to a corner it is necessary to remember that you have to move round it and absolute beginners can manage to do this still using the basic movement.

All you need to do is to dance the first half of the basic movement without turn, but then turn to the left (as described in the basic movement with turn) on the second half. If you repeat this grouping twice it will take you round the corner and you will be ready to move along the next wall; that is provided the room is rectangular in shape.

Another way of negotiating a corner is to use the right turn. Dancers often call right hand turns natural turns and similarly left hand turns reverse turns. You will come across these names later on. For the moment think only of this as the right turn. The right turn is made by taking the first four steps of the basic movement with turn to the right and then repeating these four steps.

RIGHT TURN

Man's Steps

1. Right foot forward turning body to right.	Slow
2. Left foot to side still turning to right.	Quick
3. Right foot closes to left foot still turning to right.	Quick
4. Left foot back turning to right.	Slow

5. Right foot is left forward in front of body and the
    weight is changed forward from the left foot and on
    to it (that is to say replace weight on to right foot to
    leave you standing on it) still turning to right.   Slow
6. Left foot to side still turning to right.   Quick
7. Right foot closes to left foot.   Quick
8. Left foot back.   Slow

It is possible to make quite a lot of turn to the right on these eight steps
but to start with take it easy and do not try to make too much.

Lady's Steps

1. Left foot back turning to right.   Slow
2. Right foot to side still turning to right.   Quick
3. Left foot closes to right foot still turning to right   Quick
4. Right foot forward still turning to right.   Slow
5. Left foot a small step back still turning to right.   Slow
6. Right foot to side still turning to right.   Quick
7. Left foot closes to right foot still turning to right.   Quick
8. Right foot forward.   Slow

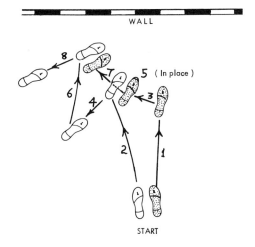

Social Foxtrot
MAN right turn

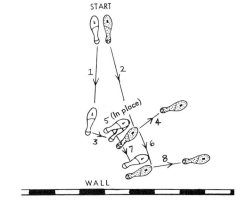

Social Foxtrot
LADY right turn

This figure, like the basic movement, can be repeated and it is possible to remain more or less on one spot on the floor and continue repeating the figure until you have turned fully round and are facing again in the direction in which you started.

At a corner it is possible to do the figure turning to the right until you are again facing towards the next wall at the end of the figure.

This figure can also follow from the end of the basic movement.

You now have two figures, the basic movement, with or without turn, and the right turn. At this stage in your lessons you must always do enough right turns to finish facing the nearest wall. Provided you do this it is then possible to follow the right turn with more right turns or with the basic movement. Of course it is possible to follow the basic movement with a set of right turns.

As a guide, you should aim to turn round one complete turn in four or less right turns.

INTRODUCTION TO CHA CHA CHA

You have learnt a little social foxtrot so now is the time to learn just one grouping in the popular cha cha cha. The music is sure to be with us for some time to come for many modern tunes are written with this rhythm. It is written with four beats to the bar. What differentiates the cha cha cha from other music written four beats to the bar is that there is a little rhythmic triplet joining the end of each bar to the next.

One bar of music can be counted for the purpose of the dance 'one, two, three, four, and'. If counted this way the counts 'four, and', fit in the time usually taken up by the count 'four' alone; that is to say they are half the time they would normally take. Two bars of music would be counted: 'one, two, three, four, and, one, two, three, four, and'.

The heavy beat is the one played at the beginning of the bar and counted 'one'. The counts at the end of the bar 'four, and' plus the first count of the next bar, the count 'one', make a little group or triplet.

It is this triplet which gives the cha cha cha much of its special sound.

In all the simple figures every time there is a 'cha cha cha count there is a little group of three steps taken called a chasse. There are two main chasses, one starting with the left and one with the right foot. Let us learn these first.

CHA CHA CHA CHASSE TO LEFT

Man's Steps

1.	Left foot small step to side.	*count* cha
2.	Right foot half closes to left foot.	cha
3.	Left foot small step to side.	Cha

Lady's Steps

1.	Right foot small step to side.	cha
2.	Left foot half closes to right foot.	cha
3.	Right foot small step to side.	Cha

(small 'c' indicates half a beat whilst capital 'C' shows that the step takes a full beat).

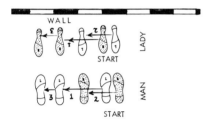

Cha Cha Cha
MAN AND LADY Chasse to left

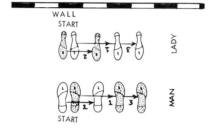

Cha Cha Cha
MAN AND LADY Chasse to right

CHA CHA CHA CHASSE TO RIGHT

Man's Steps

1.	Right foot small step to side.	cha
2.	Left foot half closes to right foot.	cha
3.	Right foot small step to side.	Cha

Lady's Steps

1.	Left foot small step to side.	cha
2.	Right foot half closes to left foot.	cha
3.	Left foot small step to side.	Cha

The music for cha cha cha is quite slow at about 32 bars per minute. Nevertheless the chasses described above move quite quickly as a result of the half beats. If you take steps which are too big you will have a real scramble. Practise each chasse until you can do it without having to think about which foot to move and in which direction. Get used to counting 'cha, cha, Cha' as you make the chasse — you can count it under your breath but count it you should.

CHA CHA CHA BASIC MOVEMENT

This is a dance which does not progress round the room which means that you may face in any direction at the start of the figure. The man holds the lady about 30 centimetres (a foot) away from himself with his right hand on the lady's back and side just above the waist. He holds the lady's right hand comfortably in his left hand at about chest level and half way between the couple.

If you have a partner you can practise first with hands on partner's shoulders, if not you can try the figure holding a chair in front of you.

Listen for the cha cha cha triplet in the music and as soon as the last cha has ended follow with the following steps:

Man's Steps

1.	Left foot forward — not a long step.	Step
2.	Right foot remains in place but weight is taken back on to it.	Step
3.	Left foot small step to side.	cha
4.	Right foot half closes to left foot.	cha

Cha Cha Cha Basic Steps 1-10

1   2   3   4   5

5. Left foot small step to side.	Cha
6. Right foot back — not a long step.	Step
7. Left foot remains in place but weight is taken forward on it.	Step
8. Right foot small step to side.	cha
9. Left foot half closes to right foot.	cha
10. Right foot small step to side.	Cha

Lady's Steps

1. Right foot back — not a long step.	Step
2. Left foot remains in place but weight is taken forward on to it.	Step
3. Right foot small step to side.	cha
4. Left foot half closes to right foot.	cha
5. Right foot small step to side.	Cha
6. Left foot forward — not a long step.	Step
7. Right foot, remains in place but weight is taken back on to it.	Step
8. Left foot small step to side.	cha
9. Right foot half closes to left foot.	cha
10. Left foot small step to side.	Cha

No doubt you have noticed that steps 3, 4 and 5 are a cha cha cha chasse as are steps 8, 9 and 10.

This figure can be repeated. It can be danced without turn but it is much better if a little turn to left is made. For beginners about four full figures to make one complete turn is suitable.

6   **7**   **8**   **9**   **10**

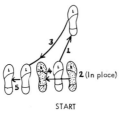

Cha Cha Cha
MAN basic movement, steps 1-5

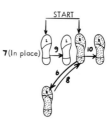

Cha Cha Cha
MAN basic movement, steps 6-10

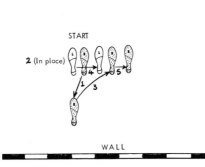

Cha Cha Cha
LADY basic movement, steps 1-5

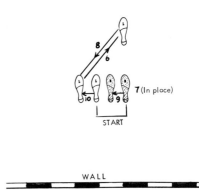

Cha Cha Cha
LADY basic movement, steps 6-10

LET'S TRY A LITTLE DISCO

Disco is a solo dance — you can dance it by yourself or with a partner — but not holding her. It is very much a fun dance, and it's easy.

This dance has not been formalised like other dances and if it had been it would tend to spoil it. What I will be doing is to try to give you the feeling for the dance so you can develop your own unique and very special dance.

Disco dances are done to a wide variety of 'beaty' music written in 4/4 time — that is with four pronounced beats to each bar of music.

Both men and ladies should now try the following preliminary exercise. Stand with the weight on the left foot now:

1.	Right foot to side — a small step.	One
2.	Pause with weight on right foot and feet apart.	Two
3.	Left foot closes to right foot, keeping weight on right foot.	Three
4.	Pause with weight on right foot but feet together.	Four
5.	Left foot to side — a small step.	One
6.	Pause with weight on left foot and feet apart.	Two
7.	Right foot closes to left foot, keeping weight on left foot.	Three
8.	Pause with weight on left foot but feet together.	Four

These steps can be repeated as often as desired. It is important to practise the steps until they can be done almost without thought. Then add the hip action which I will now describe.

1.	As right foot moves to side swing hips back a few centimetres.	One
2.	As pause is held with feet, swing hips forward a few centimetres.	Two
3.	As left foot closes to right foot (without changing weight) swing hips back a few centimetres.	Three
4.	As pause is held with feet, swing hips forward a few centimetres.	Four

Thus on the four counts given above the hips swing back, forward, back, forward. This hip action is repeated on steps 5 to 8 as described above. In addition to the hip action a little turn can be used. On steps 1 to 4 taken to the right side, a little turn to left can be used while on steps 5 to 8 a little turn to right can be used.

Since disco is danced solo the hands and arms can be moved freely. At this stage it is best to hold the hands at about waist level and forward from the body. Let the hands move naturally with the body action — keep the arms relaxed and try to forget about them.

DEFINITIONS

Dancers have a number of special expressions or phrases which they use to describe some aspects of dancing which you will need to understand. Now is the time to introduce some of them to you.

The Holds

The first ones to learn are those which relate to the way you hold your partner. The hold described in the chapter about learning earlier in the book is the hold used for most popular dances since the 1920's. It is sometimes called the 'normal' hold but I will refer to it as the closed hold showing that you stand in close proximity to your partner.

In closed hold the bodies of the couple touch — quite firmly. The lady is not absolutely central with respect to her partner. Her right hip will be somewhere in the centre of the man's hips and certainly to the man's right of his left hip.

The other important hold is that used for jive or cha cha cha and reflecting the fact that your partner is anything from 30 to 60 centimetres (a foot to two feet) apart from and facing you, is called open hold.

The man holds the lady's right hand in his left around waist height or a little higher. His right hand rests on the lady's left side or waist.

The Directions

Dancers have to understand the direction in which any step is taken relative to the room — it is assumed that the dance is taking place in a room but there are times when it could be outside — and even in a room the shape and size can vary considerably. There are rectangular ballrooms, round ballrooms and even some shaped like a letter 'L'.

For the moment consider only rectangular ballrooms shaped something like this page. You will join the dance by coming on to the dance floor from somewhere near one of the outer walls. Let us suppose that the right hand vertical edge of this page is one wall of our ballroom. You have been sitting or standing near it.

Stand with your back to the wall and you will be looking straight across the room — or if you are relating to this page of the book — to the left hand vertical edge. Enter the floor just a little way, it will depend on the size of the room, but certainly no more than a quarter of the way across the room.

Turn a right angle to your right. In the case of the page of this book you will now be facing the top short edge of the page. The wall on your right side (the long right hand vertical edge of this page) is 'the wall' to which I will be referring if I say, 'face the wall'.

Or if you stand with this wall on your right side we say you are facing 'line of dance'. If you walk forward you will soon reach a point near the corner. When you feel you are near enough then you must negotiate the corner with an appropriate figure which will be explained at a point a little later in the book. Then you are ready to move along the next line of dance which, using our analogy of the page of the book would be along the top edge.

So in a rectangular room the line of dance goes round a smaller rectangle moving in an anti-clockwise direction.

If you stand facing line of dance and then turn a right angle to your right this will leave you facing the nearest wall and this direction is called facing wall. Similarly if you face line of dance and then turn a quarter turn to left I will say you are facing inwards.

Start facing wall and then turn a right angle to right and you will have your back to the line of dance — reverting to our analogy, using the page of this book, your back will be towards the top short edge and you will be facing the bottom short edge — this is called backing line of dance.

There are two intermediate directions I shall use. If you face line of dance and turn to the right half way towards facing wall, that is half of a right angle or 45 degrees you will be facing slanting towards the wall which is called diagonally to wall. Similarly if you face the line of dance

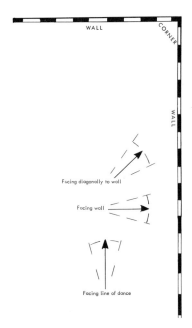

Some important directions

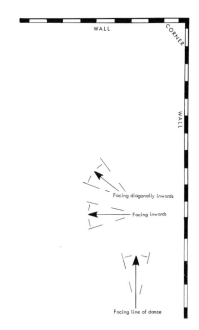

Some important directions

and turn half a right angle to left you will be facing slanting in to the room or what I will call diagonally inwards.

Body Positions

When dancing in closed hold, as in social foxtrot, waltz and so on, the partners are normally facing each other. The lady is a little to the man's right so that her right foot is not exactly pointing towards the man's left foot but is a few centimetres to the man's right — lady's left — of the position they would be in when precisely opposite each other.

This position is not maintained all the time. Sometimes the man takes a step forward placing his right foot to his left side of the lady's right foot. This sort of step is common in some dances so let us consider it in some detail. If you have a partner to practise with try this out with hands on partner's shoulders, otherwise hold a chair in front of you to get an idea of where your partner is.

It is possible to reach this special type of step from a number of different positions. Easiest, however, is to precede the special position with a step to the side on the left foot as man; lady, of course, stepping to side with the right foot. This leaves the couple standing with feet apart — say 30 to 45 centimetres (a foot to one and a half feet) — with man feeling his weight held over his left foot and lady has her weight settled on to her right foot.

The next step, as man, is to step forward with his right foot but in doing so also to cross the right foot slightly across the left foot. If the step is taken properly the insides of the right and left thighs will be pressing quite firmly together. If the step is taken in this way it will be found possible to step to the left, as man, of both your partner's feet. When you are experienced it is quite possible to do this without any other change in position but until that stage is reached you may find it helps to allow the lady's body to move a little to her left that is man's right to make sure that there is room for the step.

Steps taken in this way are taken, we say, 'outside partner'. In all simple figures there will be a step either to the side or forwards or backwards before the step taken outside partner. In the simple figures it is usually the man who is stepping forward in to the position and when he does so the lady is said to have partner outside. If the lady steps forward outside partner, as she does sometimes, then the man has partner outside.

Open Position

In many figures in dances where open hold is normal — that is the hold where man and lady do not have body contact — a position called 'open position' often happens.

When in open position the man is standing just over half a metre (about one and a half to two feet) away from partner and facing her. He holds her only with his left hand, which has hold of the lady's right hand, normally at about waist level. Do not grip the lady's hand too firmly, she will not thank you; similarly the lady's hold of the man's hand must not be too fierce.

Take care in the descriptions which follow not to confuse open hold with open position. Remember, open hold means the man will be holding partner with both hands but not in body contact. Open position refers to the relative position of the bodies and the man holds the lady with his left hand only.

Promenade Position

Another important position is called promenade position. When the man steps forward normally the lady will step back — there are times however when the man and lady will both step forward with the couple both facing roughly in the same direction. This comes about by the lady turning her right side away from the man's left side after they have been in closed hold. This leaves the couple still in body contact on the man's right and the lady's left sides but a gap between the man's left and lady's right sides.

In this position it is possible for both man and lady to step forward in the same direction. When the man steps forward on his right foot the lady will be stepping forward on her left foot and man and lady will be stepping through a space remaining between their other supporting feet, that is the man's left and lady's right foot.

It is the man's job to guide the lady to the figure — to 'lead' her. He does this by pressing on the lady's back in a rather special way with his right hand. The right hand is held on the lady's back and the bottom of the hand will be found to be near the lady's side and may even be on the lady's side. While dancing normally there is just a little pressure from the man's right hand, say enough to hold a sheet of paper against the lady's back and stop it from falling to the floor. To make the lady turn to her right to achieve promenade position the man increases the pressure from his right hand especially with the bottom (or 'heel') of the hand.

This pressure which needs to be positive without squeezing all the breath out of the lady, tells the lady (and almost forces her) to make the turn needed. Promenade position should not be achieved as a result of the man pushing forward with his left hand. This is more confusing to the lady and, as a lead, not so readily understood.

We have now reached a stage where you should be able to dance a little to something like three-quarters of the music which might be played at any function where there is dancing, other than specialised events such as Scottish dancing, old time dancing and so on.

Each of the chapters which follow will be devoted to one dance and, for example, when you have learnt the first two or three steps in the waltz you can then move to one of the other dances such as samba.

WALTZ

INTRODUCTION

The waltz is probably the most popular dance of all time. In one form or another it has been a part of the dance scene for longer than any other dance. It is amusing to reflect that it was regarded with unease and met much hostility when it was introduced.

The music is in 3/4 that is to say that there are three beats in each bar of music and the first is played with much more emphasis than the other two. This strong beat coincides with a forward or backward step in all the simple figures. In most of the simple figures one step is taken to each beat of music. Modern waltz music is played at 30 bars a minute. Danced in closed hold it is led mainly through the body.

WALTZ — closed change
(man starting right foot)

Man's Steps

1.	Right foot forward.	*Count* One
2.	Left foot to side and slightly forward.	Two
3.	Right foot closes to left foot.	Three

Lady's Steps

1.	Left foot back.	One
2.	Right foot to side and slight back.	Two
3.	Left foot closes to right foot.	Three

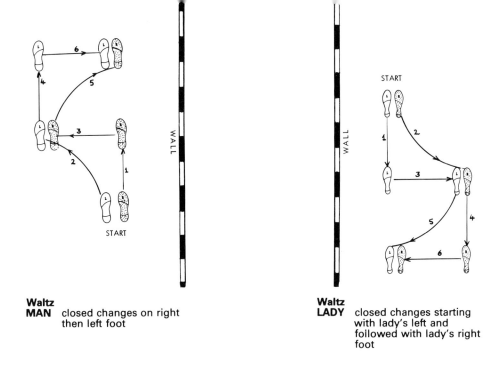

Waltz
MAN closed changes on right then left foot

Waltz
LADY closed changes starting with lady's left and followed with lady's right foot

WALTZ — closed change

(man starting left foot)

Man's Steps

1.	Left foot forward.	One
2.	Right foot to side and slightly forward	Two
3.	Left foot closes to right foot.	Three

Lady's Steps

1.	Right foot back.	One
2.	Left foot to side and slight back.	Two
3.	Right foot closes to left foot.	Three

The two change steps may be joined together one after the other and repeated as often as required. To do this the man will have to face line of dance. It is possible to move round the room doing only this so long as you curve to left when approaching a corner so as to move along the next side of the room.

QUARTER TURNS

Man's Steps

(man starts facing slanting towards the nearest wall, that is to say diagonally to wall).

1.	Right foot forward.	One
2.	Left foot to side turning to right to face wall.	Two
3.	Right foot closes to left foot making sure that you take the weight on to the right foot, continue turning to right.	Three
4.	Left foot back.	One
5.	Right foot to side.	Two
6.	Left foot closes to right foot making sure you change weight to left foot.	Three
7.	Right foot back.	One
8.	Left foot to side turning to left to face wall.	Two
9.	Right foot closes to left foot, still turning to left.	Three
10.	Left foot forward.	One
11.	Right foot to side.	Two
12.	Left foot closes to right foot.	Three

WALL

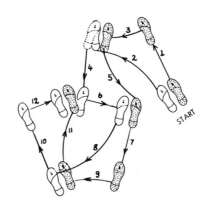

Waltz
MAN quarter turns

Lady's Steps

1.	Left foot back.	One
2.	Right foot to side, turning to right.	Two
3.	Left foot closes to right foot still turning to right and making sure to change weight on to left foot.	Three
4.	Right foot forward.	One
5.	Left foot to side.	Two
6.	Right foot closes to left foot making sure you change weight to right foot.	Three
7.	Left foot forward.	One
8.	Right foot to side, turning to left.	Two
9.	Left foot closes to right foot, still turning to left.	Three
10.	Right foot back.	One
11.	Left foot to side.	Two
12.	Right foot closes to left foot.	Three

The quarter turn in waltz may be repeated as often as desired, it can then be followed by the right or natural turn which I will now describe.

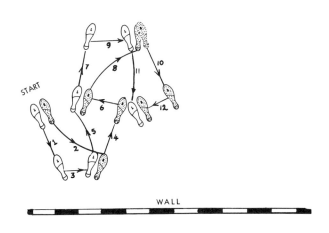

WALL

Waltz
LADY quarter turns

NATURAL TURN

(man starts facing slanting towards wall, i.e. diagonally to wall)

Man's Steps

1.	Right foot forward turning to right.	One
2.	Left foot to side still turning to right.	Two
3.	Right foot closes to left foot — now backing down room (wall on left side).	Three
4.	Left foot back turning to right.	One
5.	Right foot to side still turning to right.	Two
6.	Left foot closes to right foot now facing slanting into room, i.e. diagonally inwards.	Three

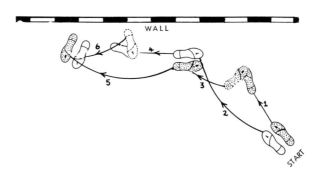

Waltz
MAN   natural (right) turn

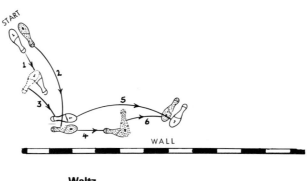

Waltz
LADY   natural (right) turn

Lady's Steps

1. Left foot back turning body to right.	One
2. Right foot to side still turning to right.	Two
3. Left foot closes to right — now facing down room.	Three
4. Right foot forward turning body to right.	One
5. Left foot to side still turning to right.	Two
6. Right foot closes to left foot — now backing slanting into room.	Three

The natural turn leaves the man facing diagonally inwards and ready to step off with his right foot. From this position he can dance a change step starting with his right foot and then the reverse (or left) turn; the description for which follows:

REVERSE TURN

Man's Steps

1. Left foot forward diagonally inwards turning body to left.	One
2. Right foot to side still turning to left.	Two
3. Left foot closes to right foot — now backing line of dance.	Three
4. Right foot back, turning body to left.	One
5. Left foot to side, still turning to left.	Two
6. Right closes to left foot — now facing diagonally outwards.	Three

Lady's Steps

1. Right foot back diagonally inwards, turning body to left.	One
2. Left foot to side, still turning to left.	Two
3. Right foot closes to left foot — now facing line of dance.	Three
4. Left foot forward, turning body to left.	One
5. Right foot to side, still turning to left.	Two
6. Left foot closes to right foot — now backing diagonally outwards.	Three

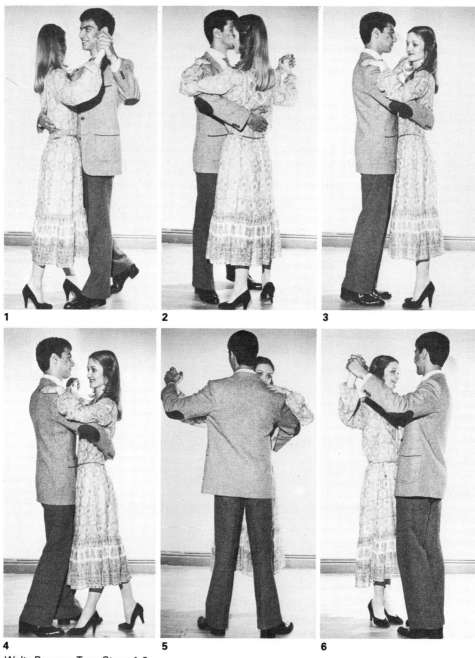

1   **2**   **3**

4   **5**   **6**

Waltz Reverse Turn Steps 1-6

42

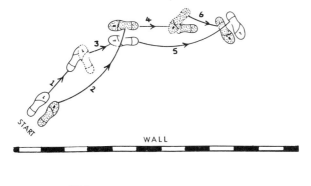

Waltz
MAN   reverse (left) turn

WALL

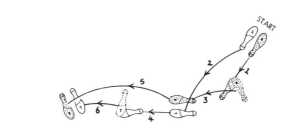

Waltz
LADY   reverse (left) turn

After the reverse turn the man is ready to step towards the wall and use his left foot. He can dance the change step starting on the left foot and then go into the natural turn or he can take the whisk immediately after the reverse turn. The whisk and chasse will be described next. This group is extremely popular and is danced by all experienced dancers.

WHISK AND CHASSE

Man's Steps
1. Left foot forward diagonally to wall.   One
2. Right foot to side and slightly forward.   Two
3. Left foot crosses behind right foot in promenade position.   Three
4. Right foot forward in promenade position along the line of dance.   One
5. Left foot to side and slightly forward along the line of dance.   Two
6. Close right foot to left foot.   and
7. Left foot to side and slightly forward.   Three

Lady's Steps
1. Right foot back diagonally to wall.   One
2. Left foot side and back commencing to turn body to right to promenade position.   Two
3. Right foot crosses behind left foot in promenade position, now facing diagonally inwards.   Three
4. Left foot forward in promenade position along line of dance.   One
5. Right foot to side, turning body to left.   Two
6. Left foot closes to right foot. Now backing diagonally to wall, and square to partner.   and
7. Right foot to side and slightly back.   Three

After the whisk and chasse the man can go into the natural turn. However, the first step of the natural turn, when taken after the chasse, is taken outside partner, that is taken with the man stepping to his left of both his partner's feet.

Instead of the natural turn the man can dance the natural spin turn, a more advanced figure and perhaps the most popular single figure in all dancing.

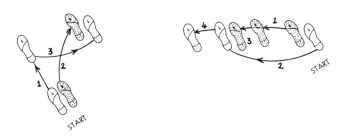

WALL

Waltz
MAN whisk steps 1-3   chasse from whisk position steps 1-4

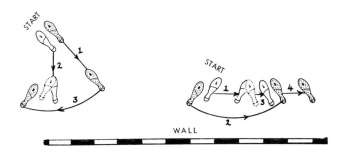

WALL

Waltz
LADY whisk steps 1-3   chasse from whisk position steps 1-4

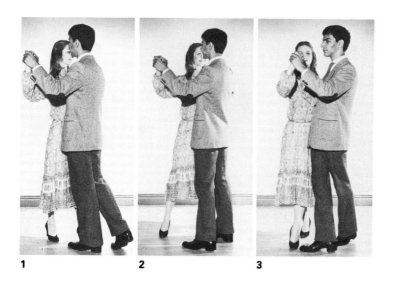

1 **2** **3**

Waltz Whisk and Chasse Steps 1-7

4 **5** **6** **7**

NATURAL SPIN TURN

This is a figure which is used extensively by all dancers and once you have mastered it you will begin to get a 'feeling' for the movement of dance. Briefly, the couple are moving round the room and then the man and his partner make a condensed turn twirling round together. You've seen it for certain.

The way to learn this figure, which calls for a little panache, is first to make quite sure that you have learnt the foot patterns and can do them without having to think too much. At this stage we find a figure where the steps for the lady are not the expected opposite of the man's. You will by now expect the lady to step back when the man steps forward and vice versa. Here at one stage the man steps forward and the lady to the side.

Try first the pattern without turn. The first three steps of the natural spin turn are those of the natural turn described earlier, so for the moment let us assume that you have done them and you are standing with your back to the line of dance as man, you should be standing feet together but with the weight firmly over the right foot. There is a pattern of three steps to learn and for these we are going to print the man's and lady's steps side by side so that you can see how they relate to each other.

Man's Steps	Lady's Steps	
1. Left foot back.	1. Right foot forward.	One
2. Right foot pushes forward a few centimetres and weight is taken forward on to it so that you are now standing on right foot only.	2. Left foot to side from right foot — feet about 30 centimetres (a foot) apart. This will bring the man's right foot more or less between the lady's feet.	Two
3. Left foot placed to side from right foot — feet about 30 centimetres (a foot) apart.	3. Right foot moves sideways and finishes to lady's left of man's left foot.	Three

47

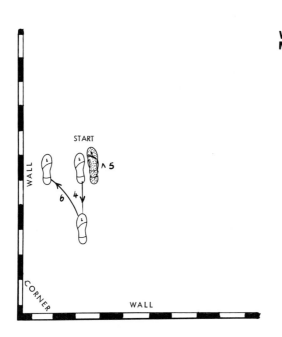

**Waltz
MAN** exercise for spin turn
(steps 4-6 of spin turn
without making turn)

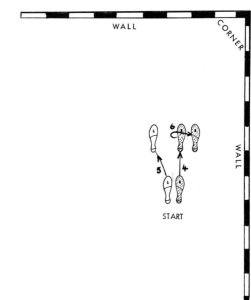

**Waltz
LADY** exercise for spin turn
(steps 4-6 of spin turn
without making turn)

48

First make sure that you have the pattern clear in your mind. For the man it is back, forward, side. For the lady it is: forward, side, side.

Now try the same pattern but turn just a little as you make the three steps. Repeat this with a little turn until it presents no difficulty. Now do it again but increase the amount of turn you make. The man starts these three steps backing line of dance and by now he should be able to face inwards across the room by the end of the third step, thus having made a 90 degrees turn. Keep practising until you can turn at least twice as much, that is to say until you can turn to face down the line of dance at the end of the three steps.

The lady too must gradually increase her turn first making sure that she can turn to face outwards towards the nearest wall having started facing down line of dance and gradually increasing the amount of turn until she can finish the three steps with her back to the line of dance.

The amount of turn indicated so far is a half turn and this is the smallest amount of turn which can reasonably be made on the three steps of the actual 'spin'. Experienced dancers will make about three-quarters of a full turn. To turn even half a turn needs a quite deliberate and conscious effort to turn strongly — indeed as the name of the figure says — to spin.

The man must hold the lady very firmly at this stage and make the positive effort to spin round taking his partner with him. It is not difficult but it does need some confidence.

There are nine steps in the full spin turn in the waltz. The pattern you have been practising is the middle group of three, that is steps 4, 5 and 6. All nine steps will now be described.

Man's Steps

(man commences facing diagonally to wall)

1.	Right foot forward.	One
2.	Left foot to side turning to right.	Two
3.	Right foot closes to left foot taking weight on to right foot when it reaches position, still turning so that man is backing line of dance.	Three
4.	Left foot back a short step turning strongly to right and keeping right foot held forward as turn is made.	One
5.	Right foot moves forward a few centimetres — as foot is moved forward it is placed between lady's feet.	Two
6.	Left foot a short step to side still turning so that man is facing diagonally to wall.	Three
7.	Right foot back.	One
8.	Left foot to side turning to left.	Two
9.	Right foot closes to left foot still turning to leave man facing diagonally inwards.	Three

This figure can now be followed by the reverse turn.

Lady's Steps

1.	Left foot back.	One
2.	Right foot to side having turned to right.	Two
3.	Left foot closes to right foot taking weight on to left foot when it reaches position, still turning to right.	Three
4.	Right foot forward a short step, turning very strongly to right.	One
5.	Left foot a short step to side, still turning strongly to right. At this point the lady steps to side and man is placing his foot forward between both the lady's feet.	Two
6.	Right foot is moved a few centimetres to side having first continued strong turn on left foot. In moving the right foot to position good dancers brush the right foot against the left foot before moving it the few centimetres to side.	Three

7. Left foot forward.   One
8. Right foot to side turning to left.   Two
9. Left foot closes to right foot taking weight on to left
   foot when it reaches position.   Three

It is possible for the man to turn more to the right on the first six steps. This will leave the man facing diagonally to wall at the end of the figure and instead of then dancing the reverse turn he will dance either a change step on left foot or a whisk.

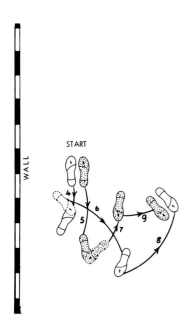

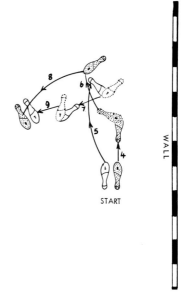

Waltz
MAN steps 4-9 of spin turn
(taken after steps 1-3
of natural turn)

Waltz
LADY steps 4-9 of spin turn
(taken after steps 1-3
of natural turn)

SAMBA

INTRODUCTION

Samba music originated in Brazil and has a tradition reaching back hundreds of years and has been associated with some voodoo religions such as Macumba. In this century first the maxixe and more recently the samba, as we know it, have been popular dances. It is a fairly easy dance redolent of the carnival atmosphere with which dancing is so often associated in Brazil.

The music can be assumed to be in 4/4 though it is often written in 2/4 time.

The steps should be learned in open position and are mostly danced this way, but in crowded conditions it is possible to dance in closed hold.

The rhythm is fairly brisk and each bar of music has three steps fitted to the bar in the figures I will describe, though there are other rhythms used by more advanced dancers. The counts for each group of three steps is 'one, a, Two'. The 'one' and the 'a' are both fitted in to the first half of the bar while the 'Two' fills the second half of the bar and takes the same time as the 'one' and the 'a' added together.

The count 'one' lasts longer than the count 'a' and since a reasonably long step is normally put to the count 'one' there is often a feeling of coming to rest on the third count 'Two'.

NATURAL BASIC MOVEMENT

(commence in close hold. May be danced with or without turn to right)

Man's Steps

1. Right foot forward.	one
2. Left foot closes to right foot.	'a'
3. Right foot remains in place and weight is transferred to it.	Two
4. Left foot back.	one
5. Right foot closes to left foot.	'a'
6. Left foot remains in place and weight is transferred to it.	Two

Lady's Steps

1. Left foot back.	one
2. Right foot closes to left foot.	'a'
3. Left foot remains in place and weight is transferred to it.	Two
4. Right foot forward.	one
5. Left foot closes to right foot.	'a'
6. Right foot remains in place and weight is transferred to it.	Two

Samba
MAN natural basic

Samba
LADY natural basic

WALL

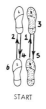

START

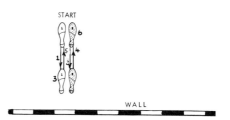

The figure may be repeated as often as you wish. The figure is described without turn but it is possible to turn a little to the right throughout — one full turn to the right can be made spread over four natural basics.

Soon you will want to change to another figure and this is done most easily by dancing the first half of the figure as described above and then following with the reverse basic. A description of this follows.

On all the figures in the samba, which I will describe — but not on all the figures in the dance itself — there is a softening or slight bending of the knees on the step counted 'one', this is followed by a straightening of the knee on the count of 'a'. The knee is bent slightly again as the weight change is made again on the count 'Two', following this the knee is again straightened, still on the count Two.

Do not overdo this action, just a little will give you the characteristic bounce action of the samba.

REVERSE BASIC MOVEMENT

(commence in close hold. May be danced with or without turn to left)

Man's Steps

1. Left foot forward.	one
2. Right foot closes to left foot.	'a'
3. Left foot remains in place and weight is transferred to it.	Two
4. Right foot back.	one
5. Left foot closes to right foot.	'a'
6. Right foot remains in place and weight is transferred to it.	Two

Lady's Steps

1. Right foot back.	one
2. Left foot closes to right foot.	'a'
3. Right foot remains in place and weight is transferred to it.	Two
4. Left foot forward.	one

5. Right foot closes to left foot.   'a'
6. Left foot remains in place and weight is transferred
   to it.   Two

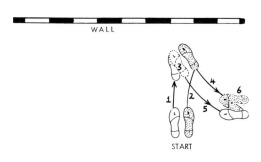

Samba
MAN reverse basic movement
(with turn)

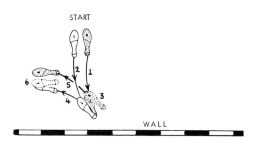

Samba
LADY reverse basic movement
(with turn)

The reverse basic can be repeated as desired. It is described without turn but turn can be made to the left. One full turn to the left can be made over four full reverse basic figures.

In order to change back to the natural basic figure this can be done after the first half of the reverse basic.

The following amalgamations of the two figures should be practised: the man should commence facing wall, dance four full natural basic movements turning to the right so that at the end of the fourth natural basic he is facing wall again; dance the forward half of the natural basic, then step forward with left foot into reverse basic movement and dance four full reverse basic movements turning to the left until man is facing wall again; now dance the forward half of the reverse basic movement.

This complete amalgamation can be repeated as often as wanted.

Both natural and reverse basics, and all other simple figures, can be danced in closed or open hold.

PROGRESSIVE BASIC MOVEMENT
(commence facing diagonally to wall)

Man's Steps
1.	Right foot forward.	one
2.	Left foot closes to right foot.	'a'
3.	Right foot remains in place and weight is transferred to it.	Two
4.	Left foot to side.	one
5.	Right foot closes to left foot.	'a'
6.	Left foot remains in place and weight is transferred to it.	Two

Lady's Steps
1.	Left foot back.	one
2.	Right foot closes to left foot.	'a'
3.	Left foot remains in place and weight is transferred to it.	Two

4. Right foot to side.   one
5. Left foot closes to right foot.   'a'
6. Right foot remains in place and weight is transferred
   to it.   Two

Samba
MAN progressive basic

Samba
LADY progressive basic

The progressive basic movement can follow the natural basic movement when it finishes facing diagonally to wall.

After the progressive basic movement the outside movement which I will describe next can be taken.

OUTSIDE MOVEMENT

Man's Steps
1.	Right foot forward.	one
2.	Left foot closes to right foot turning to left.	'a'
3.	Right foot remains in place and weight is transferred to it still turning to left.	Two
4.	Left foot back, lady stepping forward with her right foot to man's right side ie partner outside.	one
5.	Right foot closes to left foot.	'a'
6.	Left foot remains in place and weight is transferred to it.	Two
7.	Right foot forward to man's left of both lady's feet ie outside partner.	one
8.	Left foot closes to right foot turning to right.	'a'
9.	Right foot remains in place and weight is transferred to it, man should now be facing partner.	Two
10.	Left foot back.	one
11.	Right foot closes to left foot.	'a'
12.	Left foot remains in place and weight is transferred to it.	Two

Lady's Steps
1.	Left foot back.	one
2.	Right foot closes to left foot turning to left.	'a'
3.	Left foot remains in place and weight is transferred to it still turning to left.	Two
4.	Right foot forward to lady's left side of both partner's feet ie outside partner.	one
5.	Left foot closes to right foot.	'a'
6.	Right foot remains in place and weight is transferred to it.	Two
7.	Left foot back partner stepping to lady's right side of both feet ie partner outside.	one
8.	Right foot closes to left foot turning to right.	'a'

9. Left foot remains in place and weight is transferred
    to it lady now faces partner.   Two
10. Right foot forward.   one
11. Left foot closes to right foot.   'a'
12. Right foot remains in place and weight is transferred
    to it.   Two

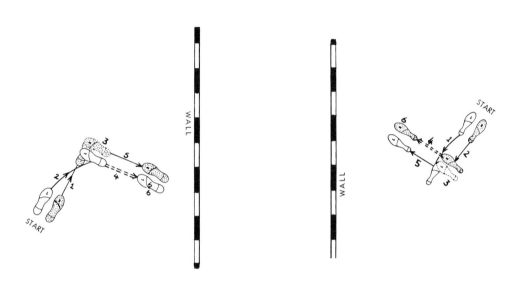

Samba
MAN outside movement
(the dotted line to the directional
arrow on step **4** indicates that
this step is taken with partner
outside)

Samba
LADY outside movement
(the dotted line on Step **4**
indicates that this step is
taken outside partner)

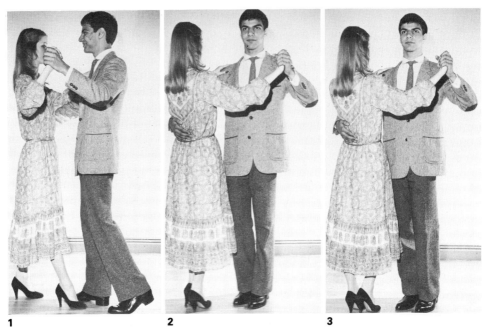

1 2 3

Samba Outside Movement Steps 1-6

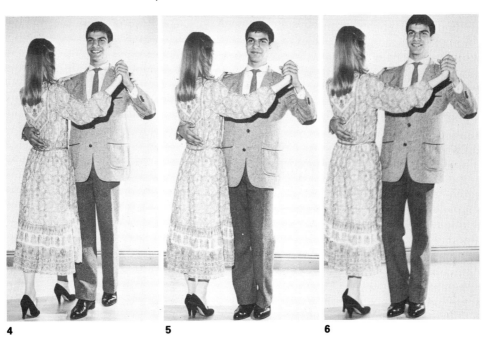

4 5 6

QUICKSTEP

For many years this was the most popular dance in the ballrooms and was regarded as the easiest by many dancers. It is danced to 4/4 music played fairly quickly. The rhythm is the same as that used for social foxtrot but is quicker.

Advanced dancers use many and exceedingly intricate patterns in this dance with many syncopated rhythms but the fundamental pleasure to be gained from the dance is created by the flow round the room.

This is another dance which uses a form of the quarter turns as the best figure with which to start your study.

QUARTER TURNS

This is the first figure in quickstep and can be repeated in the same way — with one small difference — that the quarter turns in social foxtrot and in waltz can be repeated.

The difference arises from the fact that the figure can start either in line with partner (that is with man's right foot following the lady's left foot on the first step) or outside partner (here the man's right foot does not follow the line of the lady's left foot but is placed forward to the man's left side of the lady's right foot). The description to follow will help make this clear.

The man starts facing diagonally to wall.

Man's Steps

1. Right foot forward.	Slow
2. Left foot to side turning to right to face wall.	Quick
3. Right foot closes to left foot taking weight fully on to right foot still turning to right.	Quick
4. Left foot to side a small step.	Slow
5. Right foot back.	Slow
6. Left foot to side turning to left to face wall.	Quick
7. Right foot closes to left foot taking weight fully on to right foot still turning to left.	Quick
8. Left foot to side a small step.	Slow

This ends the man's steps and he has his feet apart. To repeat the figure the first step — right foot forward — is taken by crossing the right foot slightly across the left foot and leg. This will allow the first step of the repeated quarter turns to be taken 'outside partner'.

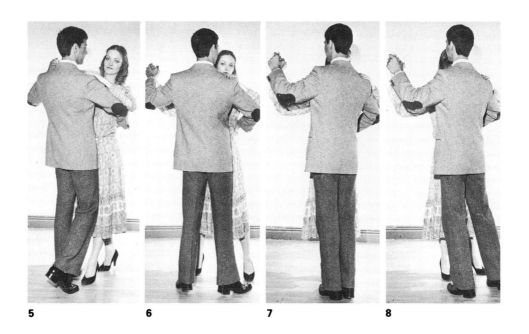

5   6   7   8

Quickstep Quarter Turns Steps 5-8
Start of second half of figure

Lady's Steps

1. Left foot back.   Slow
2. Right foot to side turning to right.   Quick
3. Left foot closes to right foot, taking weight fully on to left foot and still turning to right.   Quick
4. Right foot to side a small step.   Slow
5. Left foot forward.   Slow
6. Right foot to side turning to left.   Quick
7. Left foot closes to right foot, taking weight fully on to left foot and still turning to left.   Quick
8. Right foot to side a small step.   Slow

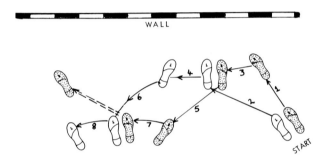

Quickstep
MAN   quarter turns including step outside partner to follow (un-numbered)

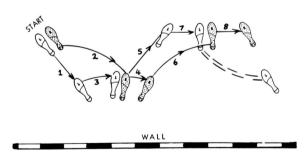

Quickstep
LADY   quarter turns including step with partner outside to follow (un-numbered)

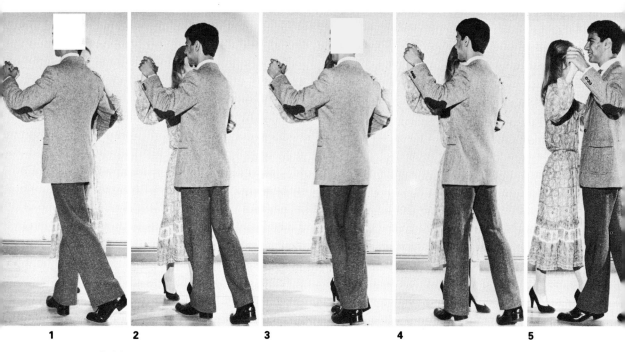

1   **2**   **3**   **4**   **5**

Quickstep Forward Lock Step — Steps 1-4
taken after step 8 of quarter turn

LOCK STEP

This figure is normally taken started outside partner and moves diagonally to wall. It follows the quarter turns very well.

Man's Steps

1. Right foot forward stepping to left of both partner's feet, that is outside partner.   Slow
2. Left foot forward turning body slightly to right.   Quick
3. Right foot crosses behind left foot — feet should not be too close together but about 15 centimetres (six inches) apart.   Quick
4. Left foot forward and a little to side, a small step. The sideways movement of the foot is to allow space to take the next step forward outside partner.   Slow

Lady's Steps

1. Left foot back, partner is stepping outside on this step.   Slow
2. Right foot back turning body slightly to right.   Quick
3. Left foot crosses in front of right foot — feet should not be too close together but about 15 centimetres (six inches) apart.   Quick
4. Right foot a short step back.   Slow

WALL

Quickstep
MAN lock step including step outside partner to follow (un-numbered)

WALL

Quickstep
LADY lock steps including step with partner outside to follow (un-numbered)

The lock step can be followed by any figure started by man stepping forward on right foot outside partner and facing diagonally to wall. So after the lock step the man can dance quarter turns or the natural turn or the spin turn. When you have learnt the quarter turns and lock step this is a good group to practise until you can dance it fairly fluently.

NATURAL TURN

This figure is described approaching the corner of the room and after the figure moving off along the next wall.

Man's Steps

1. Right foot forward, diagonally to wall, turning body to right.   Slow
2. Left foot to side, still turning to right.   Quick
3. Close right foot to left foot, still turning to right. Now backing line of dance.   Quick
4. Left foot back, turning body to right.   Slow
5. Right foot to side of left foot, small step, having turned to right on left foot, end facing diagonally to next wall.   Slow
6. Left foot forward, diagonally to wall of new line of dance.   Slow

   Note: (1) If this figure is preceded by the progressive chasse or the forward lock step, the first step will be taken outside partner.

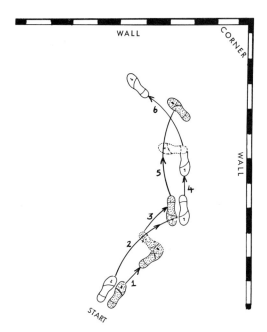

WALL

CORNER

WALL

START

Quickstep
MAN natural (right) turn

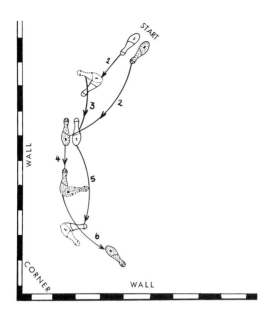

Lady's Steps

1. Left foot back, diagonally to wall, turning body to
   right. — Slow
2. Right foot to side, still turning to right. — Quick
3. Close left foot to right foot, now facing line of dance. — Quick
4. Right foot forward, turning body to right. — Slow
5. Left foot to side, still turning to right. — Slow
6. Brush right foot to left foot and then step back right
   foot. Now backing diagonally to wall of new line of
   dance. — Slow

NATURAL HESITATION TURN

This figure can be used either at a corner or along the side of the room. It is very similar to the natural turn just described. Indeed it really is only a variant of the natural turn.

By taking a wider side step on step 5 and allowing an extra 'slow' count to allow left foot to close to right foot without changing weight prior to stepping forward (as man) on step 6, you will accomplish the natural turn with hesitation. A chasse reverse turn is an excellent choice of figure to follow, when the natural hesitation turn is used along the side of the room.

CHASSE REVERSE TURN
(with progressive chasse ending)

Man's Steps

1. Left foot forward facing diagonally inwards, turning body to left. — Slow
2. Right foot to side, still turning to left. — Quick
3. Left foot closes to right foot, turning to left now backing line of dance. — Quick
4. Right foot back, turning body to left. — Slow
5. Left foot to side, still turning body to left. — Quick
6. Right foot closes to left foot — now facing diagonally to wall. — Quick
7. Left foot to side and slightly forward. — Slow

Lady's Steps

1. Right foot back diagonally inwards, turning body to left. — Slow
2. Left foot to side, still turning to left. — Quick
3. Right foot closes to left foot. Now facing line of dance. — Quick
4. Left foot forward, turning body to left. — Slow
5. Right foot to side, still turning body to left. — Quick
6. Left foot closes to right foot. Now backing diagonally to wall — Quick
7. Right foot to side and slightly back. — Slow

After the chasse reverse turn the man is facing diagonally to wall and is in a position to dance any of the figures which start in that direction on the right foot and stepping outside partner. These are the quarter turns, the lock step, the natural turn and the natural hesitation turn.

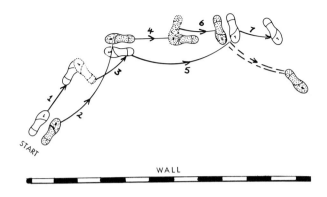

Quickstep
MAN Chasse reverse (left) turn
including step outside partner
to follow (un-numbered)

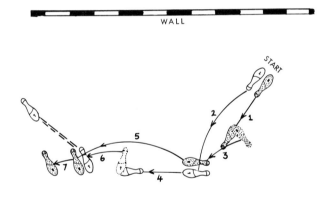

Quickstep
MAN Chasse reverse turn,
including step with partner
outside to follow (un-numbered)

JIVE

This dance is one which spans the age gap perhaps better than any other. The music is written in 4/4 time — four beats in each bar. This is the same musical time as social foxtrot but there is a difference. It is that music suitable for jive has its four beats more heavily accented and the accents are more pronounced on the second and fourth beats than the first and third.

There are generally either three steps or two taken to two beats of music. The count used will be either 'quick, a, Quick' where there are three steps or 'Quick, Quick where there are two steps.

The counts of 'quick, a' are taken in the same amount of music as the count 'Quick' with the 'quick' — with a small or lower case q at start — taking more than the count of 'a'.

Learn first the figure called basic in place, which is an excellent exercise to develop the rhythmic sense. Commence, if practising with a partner, in open hold.

BASIC IN PLACE

Man's Steps

1.	Left foot in place, take weight fully on to foot.	Quick
2.	Right foot in place, take weight fully on to foot.	Quick
3.	Left foot small step to side.	quick
4.	Right foot half closed to left foot.	'a'
5.	Left foot small step to side.	Quick
6.	Right foot small step to side.	quick
7.	Left foot half closed to right foot.	'a'
8.	Right foot to side.	Quick

Lady's Steps

1.	Right foot in place, take weight fully on to foot.	Quick
2.	Left foot in place, take weight fully on to foot.	Quick
3.	Right foot small step to side.	quick
4.	Left foot half closed to right foot.	'a'
5.	Right foot small step to side.	Quick
6.	Left foot small step to side.	quick
7.	Right foot half closed to left foot.	'a'
8.	Left foot to side.	Quick

This figure can be repeated. It should be practised until it can be danced fluently.

The basic rhythm of the figure can be used for the basic in fallaway. The basic in place can be followed by the basic in fallaway, now to be described.

BASIC IN FALLAWAY

Man faces lady in open hold and then turns towards his left and, by pushing his left hand forward slightly, guides his partner to turn to her right. This leaves man and partner turned at an angle to each other.

Man's Steps

1.	Left foot back crossing loosely behind right foot as body turns left.	Quick
2.	Right foot remains in place and weight taken forward on to it.	Quick
3.	Left foot small step to side, turning to face partner.	quick
4.	Right foot half closed to left foot.	'a'
5.	Left foot small step to side.	Quick
6.	Right foot small step to side.	quick
7.	Left foot half closes to right foot.	'a'
8.	Right foot small step to side.	Quick

Jive
MAN Basic in fallaway,
the basic steps shown on the left are steps
1-5 inclusive and those on the right are
steps 6-8 inclusive. The two halves of
the figure are shown separately to avoid
superimposition of foot patterns

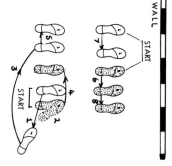

Jive
LADY Basic in fallaway the steps shown on the
left are steps 1-5 and those on the right steps 6-7.
The two halves of the figure are
shown separately to avoid
superimposition of foot patterns

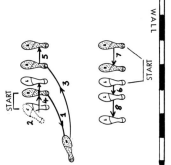

Lady's Steps

1. Right foot back crossing loosely behind left foot turns right. Quick
2. Left foot remains in place and weight taken forward on to it. Quick
3. Right foot small step to side, turning to face partner. quick
4. Left foot half closed to right foot. 'a'
5. Right foot small step to side. Quick
6. Left foot small step to side. quick

7. Right foot half closes to left foot.	'a'
8. Left foot small step to side.	Quick

LINK

(start in open hold or open position)

Man's Steps

1. Left foot back.	Quick
2. Right foot remains in place but weight taken on to it.	Quick
3. Left foot small step forward.	quick
4. Right foot closed half way to left foot.	'a'
5. Left foot remains in place but weight taken on to it.	Quick
6. Right foot small step to side.	quick
7. Left foot half closes to right foot.	'a'
8. Right foot small step to side.	Quick

Lady's Steps

1. Right foot back.	Quick
2. Left foot remains in place but weight taken on to it.	Quick
3. Right foot small step forward	quick
4. Left foot closed half way to right foot.	'a'
5. Right foot remains in place but weight taken on to it.	Quick
6. Left foot small step to side.	quick
7. Right foot half closes to left foot.	'a'
8. Left foot small step to side.	Quick

As the man steps back on the first step the lady also steps back. The man leads the lady to this back step by pushing the lady lightly away from him as he starts his step. In order to push the lady he moves his right hand so that it is more on the lady's side than normal. His right hand will leave the lady's side as she moves away from him but he retains his hold of the lady's hand in his left. The man regains his normal open hold as he takes weight forward on to the left foot at the end of the group.

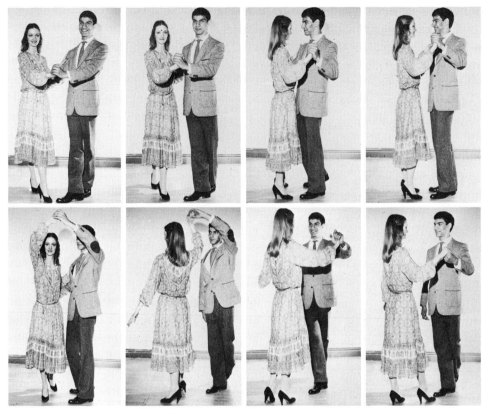

Jive, change of places right to left Steps 1-8

CHANGE OF PLACE RIGHT TO LEFT

(comence in open hold)

Man's Steps

1. Left foot back crossing loosely behind right foot, turn left.　　　　Quick

2. Right foot remains in place and weight taken forward on to it.　　　　Quick

3. Left foot small step to side.　　　　quick

4. Right foot half closed to left foot.　　　　'a'

5. Left foot small step to side lifting left hand to a height a few centimetres above lady's head and removing right hand from lady's back.　　　　Quick

6. Right foot forward turning body slightly left and allowing lady to turn to her right under arch formed by raised hands. Do not grip the lady's right hand in your left hand — you could stop her from turning altogether.   quick
7. Left foot half closes to right foot.   'a'
8. Right foot small step forward lowering left hand to waist level held in front of body.   Quick

Lady's Steps

1. Right foot back crossing loosely behind left foot.   Quick
2. Left foot remains in place but weight taken forward on to it and at same time turning to left in to man slightly.   Quick
3. Right foot small step to side still turning body slightly to left.   quick
4. Left foot half closed to right foot.   'a'
5. Right foot small step forward turning strongly to right turning back to man under raised right hand (and man's left hand).   Quick
6. Left foot between side and back still turning to right.   quick
7. Right foot half closes to left foot still turning to right.   'a'
8. Left foot small step back now facing partner and holding his left hand in your right.   Quick

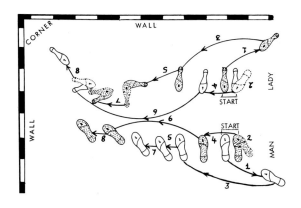

Jive
MAN AND LADY changes of places right to left

This figure leaves man holding lady's right hand in his left — facing lady and a short way away from her. Dance now either the change of place left to right which I will describe next or the link. This figure was described with man holding partner in normal position but it can be taken from open hold which is reached at the end of the change of place right to left.

CHANGE OF PLACE LEFT TO RIGHT
(commence in open position, that is as if you had just danced the change of place right to left)

Man's Steps

1.	Left foot back.	Quick
2.	Right foot remains in place and weight taken forward on to it.	Quick
3.	Left foot small step forward starting to raise left hand up and across body to guide lady to a turn to her left underneath the arch formed by her right and man's left hand. The man starts to turn to his right.	quick
4.	Right foot half closed to left foot, man's hand now above lady's head height. Man continues turn to right.	'a'
5.	Left foot small step back and side, man still turning to leave him facing partner and with left foot side of right foot.	Quick
6.	Right foot small step forward, starting to lower left arm.	quick
7.	Left foot half closed to right foot, lady now having completed turn, man's left hand back to normal height for jive.	'a'
8.	Right foot small step forward.	Quick

Lady's Steps

1. Right foot back.   Quick
2. Left foot remains in place and weight taken forward
   on to it.   Quick
3. Right foot small step forward, man is raising lady's
   right hand so she is aware that she needs to turn
   underneath the arch formed by the lady's right and
   man's left hand.   quick
4. Left foot half closed to right foot lady starting to turn
   to left.   'a'
5. Right foot small step back turning strongly to left.   Quick
6. Left foot small step back now facing partner.   quick
7. Right foot half closed to left foot.   'a'
8. Left foot small step back.   Quick

The figure finishes as it started in open position.

On the last three steps, numbers 6 to 8, the man can draw his partner towards him and finish holding her with both hands in open hold.

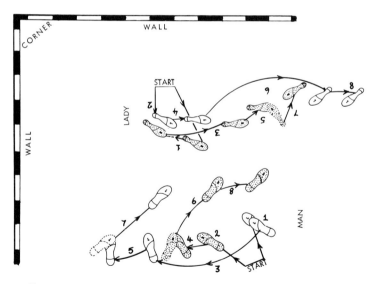

Jive
MAN AND LADY change of places left to right
(in order to ensure clarity it
has been necessary to exaggerate
the length of several steps)

CHA CHA CHA

Here is an absolutely universal dance suitable for small floors, big floors, beginners and advanced dancers. You can be smart, sophisticated and sedate while cha cha cha'ing or you can let your back hair down and really give it a whirl.

In our First Steps chapter I introduced you to the dance, now it is time to expand our repertoire. Earlier I taught the cha cha cha basic. I would now like you to try a quite exciting figure based upon the basic movement you have already mastered. If you have now mastered the basic perhaps you should check up on it again. This new figure is:

THE LADY'S SOLO RIGHT TURN

(sometimes called the under arm turn)

Man's Steps

1. Left foot forward.	Step
2. Right foot remains in place but weight is taken back on to it.	Step
3. Left foot is placed close to right foot say about 15 centimetres (six inches) away — weight is taken on to left foot when in position. Pull lady towards you slightly.	cha
4. Right foot moves towards left foot and weight is taken on to it. Start lifting left hand still holding lady's hand.	cha
5. Left foot remains in place but weight is taken on to	

78

it. Man's left hand is now above head height and continues to raise, lady is going to turn under the arch formed by the joined man's left and lady's right hand. It is important for the man not to grip the lady's hand too firmly — it will be absolutely effective in preventing her from making the turn if he does so.   Cha

6. Right foot back, left hand is now raised well clear of lady's head and starts to make a small circle in a clockwise direction, holding the lady's hand loosely in his and allowing it to turn. He is, as it were, stirring a pudding and making the lady turn quite strongly to her right.   Step

7. Left foot remains in place but weight is taken forward on to it. By now the lady will have her back towards the man.   Step

8. Right foot small step to side, lady continues her turn.   cha

9. Left foot half closes to right foot, lady still turning.   cha

10. Right foot small step to side, lady now facing man again and man lowering left hand back to starting position.   Cha

Lady's Steps

1. Right foot back.   Step

2. Left foot remains in place but weight is taken forward on to it.   Step

3. Right foot small step forward towards partner.   cha

4. Left foot half closes to right foot.   cha

5. Right foot small step forward preparing to turn to right.   Cha

6. Left foot small step to side having turned strongly to right. Turn is indicated by a lead to lady's right hand from man's left.   Step

7. Right foot remains in place and lady continues turning, her back will be roughly towards partner at this point.   Step

8. Left foot small step to side still turning so that lady's right side is now towards partner. cha

9. Right foot half closes to left foot still turning right. cha

10. Left foot small step to side still turning to right to complete turn, now facing man again. Man regains hold as at start of figure. Cha

This figure can be danced after the basic movement taught in the First Steps chapter. There is little difficulty in joining figures together in cha cha cha for all those given in this book can be taken after any other figure and they can be joined together in any sequence. There is an exception in the chasses given as an exercise in the first chapter however, they are not proper figures but merely building bricks from which figures are made.

THE FALLAWAY GROUP
(often called the hand to hand)

In this group the man changes from holding the lady's right hand in his left to holding her left hand in his right and then back to the starting hold again.

Cha Cha Cha, hand to hand Steps 1-10

Man's Steps

Dance the basic movement as described in the first lesson but as steps 8, 9 and 10 (a cha cha chasse) are taken, release hold of your partner from right hand and take hold of lady's left hand in right hand. Thus at this stage you will be holding both lady's hands in both your hands with hands held forward from the sides of the body so that there is, say, sixty centimetres (two feet) between them. As man the weight will be on the right foot. Then:

1. Left foot back a small step releasing hold of lady's right hand from your left and having turned to left so that step can be taken back side by side with partner who is also stepping back.   Step
2. Right foot remains in place but weight is taken forward on to it, body starts to turn to right.   Step
3. Left foot side small step, turning to right now nearly facing partner.   cha
4. Right foot half closes to left foot, facing partner and taking hold of lady's right hand in your left hand so that you are again holding both partner's hands in yours.   cha

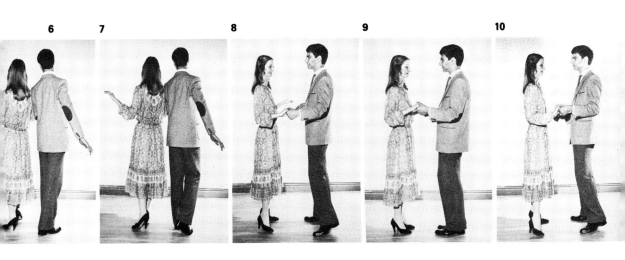

6   7   8   9   10

5. Left foot small step to side.   Cha
6. Right foot small step back releasing hold of lady's left
   hand from your right and having turned to right so
   that step can be taken back side by side with partner
   who is also stepping back.   Step
7. Left foot remains in place but weight is taken
   forward on to it, body starts to turn to left.   Step
8. Right foot small step to side, turning to left now
   nearly facing partner.   cha
9. Left foot half closes to right foot, facing partner and
   taking hold of lady's left hand in your right hand so
   that you are again holding both partner's hands in
   yours.   cha
10. Right foot small step to side, hold with both hands
    can be held when the whole figure can be repeated or
    on this step the normal cha cha cha hold can be
    regained.   Cha

Lady's Steps

(man is holding lady's left hand in his right and lady's right hand in his left at start)

1. Right foot small step back releasing hold of man's
   left hand from your right and having turned to right
   so that step can be taken back side by side with
   partner who is also stepping back.   Step
2. Left foot remains in place but weight is taken
   forward on to it, body starts to turn to left.   Step
3. Right foot small step to side, turning to left now
   nearly facing partner.   cha
4. Left foot half closes to right foot, facing partner and
   taking hold of man's left hand in your right hand so
   that you are again holding both partner's hands in
   yours.   cha
5. Right foot small step to side.   Cha
6. Left foot back a small step releasing hold of man's
   right hand from your left and having turned to left so

that step can be taken back side by side with partner who is also stepping back. **Step**

7. Right foot remains in place but weight is taken forward on to it, body starts to turn to right. **Step**

8. Left foot side small step, turning to right now nearly facing partner. **cha**

9. Right foot half closes to left foot, facing partner and taking hold of man's right hand in your left hand so that you are again holding both partner's hands in yours. **cha**

10. Left foot small step to side. **Cha**

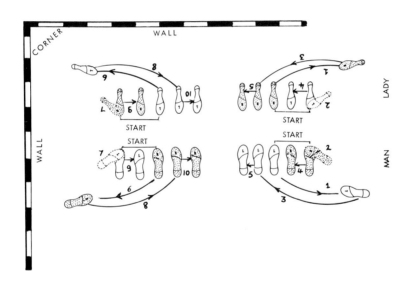

Cha Cha Cha
MAN AND LADY fallaway group,
the lower half of the steps are
1-5 inclusive while the upper half
are steps 6-10 inclusive.
The foot patterns are shown this way
to avoid superimposition of the
patterns.

NEW YORK GROUP

(This group has a long technical name not given here)

Man's Steps

(start facing wall, in open hold)

1.	Left foot forward — not a long step.	Step
2.	Right foot remains in place but weight is taken back on to it.	Step
3.	Left foot small step to side.	cha
4.	Right foot half closes to left foot starting to turn body to left and to turn lady to her right.	cha
5.	Left foot small step to side turning left side of body further away from partner and turning partner further to her right by pushing forward a little with left hand. Couple are now in promenade position.	Cha
6.	Right foot small step forward in promenade position partner stepping forward in same direction. Man and lady now facing line of dance approximately.	Step
7.	Left foot remains in place but weight is taken back on to it, body starts to turn to right towards partner.	Step
8.	Right foot small step to side, man having first turned to right to face partner and taking right hand from partner's side, that is releasing hold with right hand.	cha
9.	Left foot half closes to right foot man still turning right. The natural action of man's left hand when following the man's turn will turn the lady to her left. Man holds lady's right hand in his left.	cha
10.	Right foot small step to side, man continuing his turn to right. Lady will continue turning to her left and both partners will be facing nearly in the same direction, man's left side will be towards lady's right side, and man and lady will have their backs to line of dance.	Cha
11.	Left foot forward small step, lady is also stepping forward (with her right foot) and the nearest wall is on both man's and lady's left side.	Step

12. Right foot remains in place but weight is taken back on to it.   Step

13. Left foot small step to side man having first turned to left to face partner, the movement of the man's left arm will cause lady to turn her right to face man. Man lifts right hand and takes hold of lady's left hand in it.   cha

14. Right foot half closes to left foot, man still turning to his left, and lady to her right.   cha

15. Left foot small step to side, letting go of lady's hand with left hand. Man is now holding lady's left hand in his right hand and both are facing towards the line of dance.   Cha

16. Right foot small step forward, in side by side position with partner both facing line of dance.   Step

17. Left foot remains in place but weight is taken back on to it.   Step

18. Right foot small step to side having turned to right towards partner. Action of man's right arm in turn will cause lady to turn to her left towards partner.   cha

19. Left foot half closes to right foot, now facing partner, take hold of partner's side and back again with right hand — normal hold.   cha

20. Right foot small step to side now facing partner and back in normal hold.   Cha

Note: It is not essential that the holds change exactly at the points given — a step out will make little difference.

Lady's Steps

(start backing wall)

1. Right foot back — not a long step.   Step

2. Left foot remains in place but weight is taken forward on to it.   Step

3. Right foot small step to side.   cha

4. Left foot half closes to right foot starting to turn body to right.   cha

5. Right foot small step to side turning right side of body further away from partner, now in promenade position.   Cha

6. Left foot small step forward in promenade position partner stepping forward in same direction. Man and lady both facing approximately to line of dance.   Step

7. Right foot remains in place but weight is taken back on to it. Body starts to turn to left towards partner.   Step

8. Left foot small step to side, turning to left to face partner, man will release hold on lady's back and side from his right hand.   cha

9. Right foot half closes to left foot still turning body to left.   cha

10. Left foot small step to side, continuing turn so that lady and man are now both facing nearly in the same direction. Lady's right and man's left sides will be towards each other.   Cha

11. Right foot forward small step.   Step

12. Left foot remains in place but weight is taken back on to it.   Step

13. Right foot small step to side having first turned to right to face partner. Man will take hold of lady's left hand in his right.   cha

14. Left foot half closes to right foot, still turning to right.   cha

15. Right foot small step to side, now facing in same direction as man, towards line of dance.   Cha

16. Left foot small step forward in side by side position with partner, both facing line of dance.   Step

17. Right remains in place but weight is taken back on to it.   Step

18. Left foot small step to side having turned to left towards partner.   cha

19. Right foot half closes to left foot, now facing partner,

man will regain normal hold.   cha

20. Left foot small step to side now facing partner and
     back in normal hold.   Cha

The shortest version of this figure has been described — it is possible
having danced steps 1 to 15 to follow with steps 6 to 15 again before
moving on to step 16.

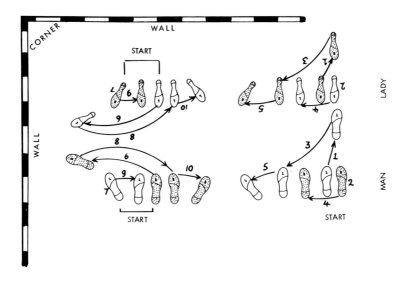

Cha Cha Cha
MAN AND LADY New York Group steps 1-10 only.
Shown in two halves to avoid superimposition
of the patterns.

DISCO

This is the most popular current dance. It is very much a dance of youth, but there is no reason why older generations should not enjoy the dance and many now do.

Every public dance session is likely to devote a substantial part of the evening to disco. The dances were developed in discotheques. They are mainly danced solo and it is the solo dances that I will teach.

Being a solo dance it is very much a free style dance with each dancer developing his own form of expression. It is often very energetic but does not need to be so. You should try to do your own thing as far as possible and use the figures I will teach as a basis on which you can enlarge.

The beats in the music are very heavily accented or marked. There are four in each bar of music (4/4 time) and the rhythm is one which is very hard to miss.

HIP THRUSTS (OR BUMPS)

Man and Lady
(start with feet slightly apart and weight felt on left foot)

1. Left foot remains in place and hips are thrust sharply leftwards and then back to right to starting position.　One
2. Left foot remains in place and previous 'step' is repeated by thrusting hips first to left and then out to normal position again.　Two
3. Right foot remains in place but weight is taken on to it and hips are thrust sharply rightwards and then back to normal position.　Three

4. Right foot remains in place and hips thrust again first rightwards and then back to normal.   Four

The figure should be danced with hands held about waist level to start with. It is possible to repeat steps 1 and 2 before moving on to steps 3 and 4, in which case 3 and 4 should also be repeated.

Using the above hip actions and adding the foot patterns given below creates the basic disco group.

DISCO BASIC
1. Left foot a short step to side turning slightly right.   One
2. Right foot moves towards left foot and taps on floor.   Two
3. Right foot a short step to side turning slightly left.   Three
4. Left foot moves towards right foot and taps on floor.   Four

Repeat this group using the hip thrusts at the same time as often as you want.

As well as the hips, hands and arms are used in disco and the simplest use is to clap.

BASIC WITH CLAPS
1. No hand action.   One
2. Clap hands together as right foot taps on floor.   Two
3. No hand action.   Three
4. Clap hands together as left foot taps on floor.   Four

Another hand action is that called:
THE HITCH HIKER
(to disco basic foot pattern)
1. Left foot moves to side and right hand, fingers bent thumb raised, is swung over right shoulder as if thumbing a lift.   One
2. Right foot taps to floor and thumbing action with right hand is repeated.   Two
3. Right foot moves to side and thumbing action with

| Disco | Hitch Hiker weight on left foot | Disco | Hitch Hiker weight on right foot | Disco | Roly Poly weight on left foot |

left hand is made over left shoulder. Three

4. Left foot taps to floor and thumbing action with left
   hand is repeated. Four

ROLY-POLY HAND ACTIONS

This hand and arm action can also be used while dancing the disco basic and has the virtue that there is no set rhythm to which it should be done.

The hands and arms are held in the position you would reach just before crossing your arms; the forearms are roughly parallel to the floor, the right hand pointing leftwards and the left hand pointing rightwards. Let us suppose the right arm is nearer the body then the left. Lift the right arm a few centimetres and then move it forward — while doing this lower the left arm a few centimetres and then move it back towards the body. The right arm will pass over the top of the left arm. Now bring the right arm back under the left arm to both their original positions. This is one roly-poly action. It is done quickly and repeated several times.

With these few foot, hip and arm actions you should be ready to venture on to any disco floor. Remember, try to listen to and absorb the music and let your own natural responses develop.

MORE SOCIAL FOXTROT

In Chapter 2 I introduced you to social foxtrot but the figures given do not give much variety. So the following groups should now be learnt to enlarge your dance 'vocabulary'.

SIDE STEP

Man's Steps

1. Left foot to side. — Quick
2. Right foot closes to left foot keeping the weight on the left foot, that is keep standing on the left foot. — Quick
3. Right foot to side. — Quick
4. Left foot closes to right foot keeping the weight on the right foot. — Quick
5. Left foot to side. — Quick
6. Right foot closes to left foot this time and standing on the right foot. — Quick
7. Left foot forward. — Slow

Lady's Steps

1. Right foot to side. — Quick
2. Left foot closes to right foot keeping the weight on the right foot. — Quick
3. Left foot to side. — Quick
4. Right foot closes to left foot keeping the weight on the left foot. — Quick
5. Right foot to side. — Quick

6. Left foot closes to right foot this time and standing
   on the left foot.   Quick
7. Right foot back.   Slow

The side step can follow the seventh step of the quarter turns and can be followed by the quarter turns or the natural turn.

Steps 1 to 6 of the side step can be repeated. If you relax and absorb the music rhythmic action in the knees should become evident and you will feel you want to bend the supporting knee just a little on the second and fourth step of the side step. This is right and you should encourage the feeling.

REVERSE TURN

The social foxtrot reverse turn is the second half of the quarter turns repeated (as the natural turn is the first half repeated).

Man's Steps

(after step 4 of the quarter turn)
1. Right foot back starting to turn to left.   Slow
2. Left foot small step to side still turning left.   Quick
3. Right foot closes to left foot still turning left.   Quick
4. Left foot forward — do not take too long a step and
   leave right foot in position.   Slow
5. Right foot back a few centimetres from position it is
   in, still turning left.   Slow
6. Left foot small step to side still turning left.   Quick
7. Right foot closes to left foot still turning left.   Quick
8. Left foot forward.   Slow

The figure may be repeated as often as wished or it can be followed with the quarter turns or the right or natural turn. In the reverse turn the turn is not a strong turn and at least four groups of four steps should be used to turn one full turn.

Lady's Steps

1. Left foot forward starting to turn to left.   Slow
2. Right foot small step to side still turning left.   Quick

3. Left foot closes to right foot still turning left.   Quick
4. Right foot back — do not take too long a step and
   leave left foot in position.   Slow
5. Left foot forward a few centimetres from position it is
   in still turning left.   Slow
6. Right foot small step to side still turning left.   Quick
7. Left foot closes to right still turning left.   Quick
8. Right foot back.   Slow

WALL

Social Foxtrot
MAN   reverse turn

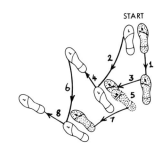

Social Foxtrot
LADY   reverse turn

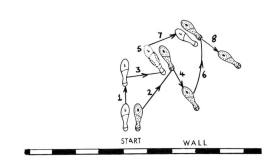

93

TAILPIECE

I hope you have been successful in mastering the dances contained in this book. In most towns you will find schools of ballroom dancing where you will be able to enlarge your repertoire. If you would like a list of such schools run by qualified dance teachers it can be obtained free of charge from:

The International Dance Teachers Association
76 Bennett Road
Brighton
BN2 5JL